CONCORD

JUL 2 4 2008

D0572960

CONCEPT

Art Profiles
For Kids

PIERRE-AUGUSTE RENOIR

WITHDRAWN

CONTRA COSTA COUNTY LIBRARY

Mitchell Lane
PUBLISHERS

P.O. Box 196
Hockessin, Delaware 19707

Visit ⬚⬚⬚⬚⬚⬚⬚⬚e.com
Commen⬚⬚⬚⬚⬚⬚⬚⬚⬚⬚elllane.com

3 1901 04311 6385

ART PROFILES FOR KIDS

Titles in the Series

Art Profiles
For Kids
PIERRE-AUGUSTE RENOIR

Barbara Somervill

P.O. Box 196
Hockessin, Delaware 19707
Visit us on the web: www.mitchelllane.com
Comments? email us: mitchelllane@mitchelllane.com

Copyright © 2008 by Mitchell Lane Publishers. All rights reserved. No part of this book may be reproduced without written permission from the publisher. Printed and bound in the United States of America.

Printing   1   2   3   4   5   6   7   8   9

Library of Congress Cataloging-in-Publication Data
Somervill, Barbara A.
    Pierre Auguste Renoir / by Barbara Somervill.
       p. cm. — (Art profiles for kids)
    Includes bibliographical references and index.
    ISBN 978-1-58415-566-9 (library bound)
    1. Renoir, Auguste, 1841–1919—Juvenile literature. 2. Painters—France—Biography—Juvenile literature. I. Renoir, Auguste, 1841–1919. II. Title.
ND553.R45S66 2007
759.4—dc22
                                                                                              2007000661

ABOUT THE AUTHOR: **Barbara Somervill** is a working writer and a lifelong learner. Her writing has taken her through several careers: journalism, teaching, drama, corporate communications, educational textbook writing, and nonfiction children's writing. Ms. Somervill has had more than 75 books published. This is her first book for Mitchell Lane Publishers. Ms. Somervill is an avid bridge player and loves theater and reading. She lives in South Carolina with her husband and is a mother and grandmother.

ABOUT THE COVER: The images on the cover are paintings by the various artists in this series.

PHOTO CREDITS: p. 6—Christie's Images/Superstock; p. 34—Hulton Archive/Getty Images; all other images are the works of Pierre-Auguste Renoir.

PUBLISHER'S NOTE: The facts on which this story is based have been thoroughly researched. Documentation of such research appears on page 46. While every possible effort has been made to ensure accuracy, the publisher will not assume liability for damages caused by inaccuracies in the data, and makes no warranty on the accuracy of the information contained herein.

PLB

Table of Contents

Art Profiles for Kids

The Bathers (1892) sold at an auction in 1998 for over $3.4 million. Renoir painted several versions of women bathing in pools.

one

A Painter's Legacy

Anxious bidders gathered at Sotheby's auction house. The items for sale that spring day in 1998 were art works by Impressionists and modern artists, including Claude Monet (MOH-nay), Gustave Caillebotte (kye-BAHT), Marc Chagall (shuh-GAHL), and, of course, Pierre-Auguste Renoir (pee-AIR oh-GOOST rehn-WAHR). No Impressionist auction would have been complete without a few offerings from the brilliant Renoir.

A hush flowed through the audience. Bidders waited for Lot Six. The auctioneer cleared his throat.

Lot Six was an oil painting, *Baigneuses*, or *The Bathers*, by Renoir. As most Impressionist fans know, women bathing in the open air was a common Renoir theme.

This particular canvas measures eighteen and one-eighth inches by fifteen inches. It is a charming painting of two girls in sunbonnets watching several other young women swim. Few Renoirs of this size show the same attention to detail or clear colors as *Baigneuses*.

The bidding began. Numbered paddles shot up—bidding was brisk. Finally, a bid came in at nearly $3.5 million, followed by silence. The auctioneer asked, "Any advance on $3,412,500? If not, I'm selling." With a single rap of his gavel, the Renoir became the property of a proud new owner. For nearly $3.5 million, the purchaser bought a painting that is about the size of a closed laptop computer.

The price for this work was not unusual. Small Renoir oil paintings regularly sell for sums upward of $1 million. Even numbered prints signed by the artists can bring more than $10,000, even though there may be dozens of each lithograph still in existence. A museum-size, museum-quality piece, such as *The Swing* or *The Luncheon of the Boating Party*, rarely comes up at auction. A Renoir of that quality is far too valuable for a museum to part with.

If Pierre-Auguste Renoir were alive today, he would laugh at the idea that his art brought such a remarkable sum. Although he earned a good living from his painting, he never received anywhere near the equivalent of $10,000 per piece, let alone $3.4 million.

He might joke about the time that he painted a woman's portrait in exchange for a pair of shoes. She wanted a portrait; he really needed the shoes. He might have remarked that he began his artistic career painting flowers on dishes or pretty pictures on ladies' fans. He was paid by the piece, a few cents for a bouquet and a few more for a portrait. Renoir earned a decent living doing commercial art, but he gave up the steady, sure income for the risky business of fine art.

Renoir would have definitely pointed out that at one early Impressionist exhibition in 1874, he earned a total of 18 francs. That pitiable sum did not even keep him in paint and canvas. And with some embarrassment, he would admit that during those rough years, he begged his friends for rent money. "M. Duret [doo-REY]," Renoir wrote, "I have a payment to make this morning. Can you let me have something or tell me when and what amount so that I could make an exact promise? . . . I should be very grateful to you for not forgetting me this month because I am in a bottomless pit."[1] Being broke was a constant condition for Renoir and his Impressionist friends in the 1870s.

Even more surprising to Renoir than the price earned by his art would have been the auctioneer describing him as a brilliant artist. It was a term he never used for himself. He preferred to call himself a "workman painter." Renoir's massive art output speaks more to production line than an artist's studio. During his lifetime, he produced more than 5,000 paintings and a similar number of sketches, charcoals, pastels, and watercolors. With more than 10,000 works to his credit, Renoir created roughly 170 pieces of art yearly over nearly 58 years.

Renoir truly sweated at his craft, developing his skills throughout his life. He was friends with many popular artists of his day and learned from them. For example, Virgilio Diaz de La Peña (veer-HEE-lee-oh DEE-az-de-lah-PAYN-yah) taught Renoir to avoid black paint and dull colors. Courbet (cor-BAY) encouraged Renoir to stay close to real life in his topics. Corot (caw-ROH) promoted the idea of including nature in art.

In addition to learning through friends, Renoir also said that an artist learns through studying the great masters. "It's in the museums that one learns to paint," Renoir said. ". . . it is in the museums that [an artist] acquires the taste for painting that nature alone can never give. It isn't a pretty view that makes one want to be a painter, it's a picture."[2]

Renoir's paintings are generally cheerful, uplifting, and positive. There are no depressing, gory, or revolting Renoirs. Renoir didn't believe in it. He said, "To my mind, a picture should be something agreeable, cheerful and—yes!—nice to look at. There are too many nasty things in the world as it is, without our adding to them. I know that few people are prepared to admit that a painting can really be first-class and cheerful at the same time."[3] French art critic Octave Mirbeau (ahk-TAHV meer-BOW) once said that Renoir "lived and painted. He pursued his craft. . . . As such, his entire life and his work are lessons in happiness."[4]

In his youth, Renoir struggled to make ends meet and often went into debt to pay his rent or buy art supplies. By the time he married, however, he earned a decent income and supported his family comfortably. He was a devoted husband to Aline (ah-LEEN) and father to his three sons, and he thoroughly enjoyed family life. Renoir was humble about his work and never showed the kind of bloated, overbearing ego that often comes with success.

Because of Renoir's fame, lesser artists copied his work and sold forgeries as originals. Renoir hated seeing people cheated, particularly over his art. As an old man, he told about a retired army officer who thought he had bought a Renoir. The officer told Renoir that he purchased one of the artist's pictures. The officer used all his savings and took out loans against his home and pension to make the purchase. Renoir looked at the work and knew

Originally established by Napoléon Bonaparte, the French Legion of Honor is an important award in France. Not a person to be impressed by awards, Renoir was almost embarrassed to receive the Legion of Honor medal.

immediately that it was a forgery. He said nothing but told the man to leave the picture with him so that he could touch it up a bit. Renoir repainted the picture, signed it, and returned it to the man. That officer never knew that the picture he bought was a forgery, only that he was the proud owner of a Renoir. That simple act of kindness was typical of Renoir's attitude toward life: open-minded, modest, and generous.

On August 16, 1900, Pierre-Auguste Renoir received word that he had been named chevalier of the Legion of Honor. This highest of French honors is similar to an English knighthood or the American Medal of Honor. Typical of Renoir, he was somewhat embarrassed by the fuss. He did not even go to the ceremony, sending an agent to pick up his award.

The Legion of Honor award bothered Renoir. He worried what his longtime friend Claude Monet would think. Monet opposed all honors and poked fun at those who received them. Upon hearing of the honor, Renoir immediately sent a letter of apology to Monet: "I let them decorate [honor] me. Be assured that I am not letting you know to tell you whether I am wrong or right, but so that this little piece of ribbon does not become an obstacle to our old friendship."[5] This was Renoir at his best. He received an honor that would make most men brag, yet his first concern was that he should not lose a friend because of it. A national honor was, after all, little more to Renoir than a "little piece of ribbon."

Impressionism

Impressionism was a major movement that developed mainly in France during the late nineteenth century. The idea behind Impressionism was to break with classical art styles and create "impressions" on canvas.

The first artists to look into the idea of Impressionism were Eugene Boudin (yoo-ZHEN boo-DAHN), Stanislas Lepine (leh-PEEN), and Johan Jongkind (YUNG-kihnd). Boudin met Claude Monet when Monet was only fifteen. He taught Monet to observe the effects of sunlight on the Seine River. Monet learned to paint the light, a characteristic found in most Impressionist art.

Several years later, Monet became friends with Alfred Sisley, Camille Pissarro, and Pierre-Auguste Renoir. These artists, along with Edgar Degas (day-GAH), Paul Cézanne (say-ZAHN), and Berthe Morisot (mor-ree-SOH), rejected the formal, stilted painting of Paris' École des Beaux-Arts (School of Fine Arts). Instead, they produced art with a freer, less defined style. Their theory of art was that color should be dropped directly on a canvas. From the early 1860s, these artists approached art with a new energy. They began painting *en plein air* (in open air) to study light and its effects on nature.

Monet Reading (1872) by Renoir

The name for the art movement came from a painting by Monet called *Impression: Sunrise*, painted in 1872. Being called an Impressionist was not a compliment. Art critics, art dealers, and art academies openly rejected the new form. Impressionist paintings were regularly refused space in the Salon, a prestigious exhibit held yearly in Paris.

By the late 1880s, Impressionism was dying. The Impressionists were getting older. All but Monet mellowed and produced art that was easier to sell. In the twentieth century, art critics changed their thinking and claimed that Impressionism was the most important artistic movement of the nineteenth century. Today, when works by Monet or Renoir are sold at auction, they can bear a multimillion-dollar price tag.

After coffee, several men discuss what is in the news in Renoir's *At the Inn of Mother Anthony* (1866). The newspaper is *The Event*, the paper that featured reviews of the first salons held by the Impressionists.

Learning His Craft

Pierre-Auguste Renoir was born on February 25, 1841, in the small town of Limoges (lee-MOHZH), France. Although his name was officially Pierre-Auguste, he was called Auguste. His mother, Marguerite, claimed that *Pierre Renoir* had simply too many r's and was too hard to pronounce.

The Renoir family in 1841 consisted of father Léonard, mother Marguerite, and three older children: Pierre-Henri (called Henri), Marie-Elisa (called Lise), and Léonard-Victor (called Victor). Léonard earned his living as a tailor; his wife was a seamstress. By 1845, Léonard's tailoring business was struggling, and he decided to move the family to Paris. The family settled into a small apartment in a rundown area near the Louvre (LOOV), a famous art museum.

The Paris of Renoir's youth was very different from the major city that Paris is today. In the Paris of 1845, few people had hot and cold running water. Those who could afford it bought water from water wagons. Those with little money filled their water jugs from central city fountains. Along with the lack of running water, Paris had no sewage system. People relieved themselves in chamber pots and emptied the pots out the window or into the Seine River. Bathing was a rare event, since collecting and heating enough water for a bath took tremendous effort, and what was the point? No one else bathed regularly.

No Parisian had central heating, depending instead on open coal or wood fires. Many people contracted diseases such as tuberculosis, diphtheria, and whooping cough. A high percentage of children died before their first birthday. The Renoirs, like other Parisians, purchased their food in market gardens, grew vegetables in their backyard, and bought meat and sausage from the local butchers. Bakers sold coarse, whole-grain breads and pastries. There were no refrigerators, so food was purchased and eaten on the same day. Shopping was a daily chore.

As a child, Auguste played marbles with other children in his neighborhood. Although the Renoirs lived in a slum, their neighborhood was close to the palace in which the royal family lived. France's Queen Marie-Amélie's apartments overlooked the streets surrounding the Louvre. She often threw candy from her window to Auguste Renoir and his friends.

The Renoir apartment served as both living quarters and tailor's workshop. Léonard sewed suits, shirts, and pants for his customers in the front room. At night, he cleared away his scissors, needles, pins, fabrics, and tailor's chalk from his workbench. That same bench became Auguste's bed—and Auguste's biggest problem at the time was stepping barefoot on pins his father carelessly left on the floor. Papa Renoir's tailor's chalk became Auguste's first art medium. He drew portraits of his family and neighbors in chalk on the apartment's wooden floor.

When not playing with his friends, Auguste attended school. The French government provided free schools, and Auguste headed off to one run by Christian brothers. French schools taught reading, writing, and mathematics. Unruly students were rapped on their hands with rulers. In the winter, classrooms were bitterly cold. The education may have been free to the parents, but the students paid dearly for what they learned.

Auguste's favorite time in school was when they sang. He had a marvelous voice and began singing in the boys' choir of St. Eustache Church. Renoir's voice was so fine that he could have received a scholarship to study music. However, his father disagreed. He had grown up in Limoges and respected the artistry of painting porcelain dishes—which was the primary industry of the town. Léonard Renoir apprenticed Auguste to the Lévy brothers' porcelain studio.

In 1854, at the age of thirteen, Auguste Renoir began painting dishes, vases, and other china at the Lévys'. He received payment by the piece, two sous for a dessert plate and three sous for a portrait of Marie Antoinette. Eventually, Renoir made a reasonably good living. "I had been able to help my parents buy a house out at Louveciennes, to which they could retire some day. I could even have lived independently of them—and at fifteen, that isn't doing badly. But I liked talking with my mother at home in the evening."[1]

Unfortunately, the Levys' business went bankrupt in 1858. The Industrial Revolution had brought changes to the china industry. A new machine stamped pictures on dishes, vases, and bowls far more quickly than an artist could paint them. Renoir had to find another way to make money, and he shifted from china to ladies' fans and window blinds. To add to his income, he painted decorations on café walls.

Renoir used his lunch hours to study paintings displayed in the Louvre Museum. He analyzed the works of Peter Paul Rubens, Jean-Honoré Fragonard, François Boucher, and Jean-Antoine Watteau. In his free time, he sketched figures based on the pictures he studied. Like painting porcelain and fans, these sketches were Renoir's informal art school.

Within three years, Renoir entered the Gleyre (GLAYR) studio, an art class run by an old Swiss painter, Charles Gleyre. The studio began Renoir's life as a serious artist. There were thirty or forty students there, including Monet, Frédéric Bazille, and Alfred Sisley.

Once, Gleyre viewed a canvas on which Renoir was working. The teacher commented, "You paint for your own amusement, I suppose?"

"Well, of course!" replied Renoir. "If it didn't amuse me, I assure you that I wouldn't paint at all."[2] Gleyre was not amused. He felt that painting should be serious, technical, and defined. For Renoir, painting was more than a way of earning a living. It was his personal joy.

In 1862, Renoir took the admission test for the École des Beaux-Arts. He squeaked out a passing grade, coming in sixty-eighth out of eighty hopeful students. Renoir later said, "I was a hard-working student; I ground away at academic painting; I studied the classics, but I did not obtain the least honorable mention, and my professors were unanimous in finding my painting [terrible]."[3]

Renoir remained committed to his art, studying at both the academy and Gleyre's studio. In 1864, Gleyre retired, but the dedicated artists in his studio continued to study without a teacher. At the academy, Renoir submitted a

Renoir often used Lise Tréhot as a model for his work between 1865 and 1872. Renoir was spending the spring with other friends who were painters when he produced *Lise with a Parasol* (1867). This painting shows how well Renoir could capture light. The dress is airy, soft, and flowing, while the black ribbon train reflects the sunlight.

picture to the annual competition, called the Salon. The Salon was a panel of judges from the academy who selected 2,500 pictures each year for an exhibition. Renoir's *Esmeralda Dancing with a Goat* was accepted. However, many of his friends did not have pictures exhibited. They put on their own exhibition, called the *Salon des Réfuses*—a show for pictures that had been refused for the official exhibit.

While attending art school and studying with Gleyre, Renoir became close friends with Claude Monet, Alfred Sisley, and Jean Frédéric Bazille. The four artists took a trip to Chailly-en-Bière to paint nature studies. Painting *en plein air* (in open air) was a change from earlier landscape painting. In the past, an artist sketched scenes outdoors but always painted in a studio. One day while painting *en plein air*, artist Virgilio Diaz de La Peña looked over Renoir's work and asked him why he used so much black paint. Diaz de La Peña told Renoir to give up black and paint the light. Renoir's art changed from the dark, somber blacks of *At the Inn of Mother Anthony* to the bright whites of *Lise with a Parasol*, painted in 1867.

Claude Monet

Claude Monet (1840–1926) is known throughout the world as an artistic creator and the father of Impressionism. In fact, Impressionism's name came from a Monet work, *Impression: Sunrise*, painted in 1872.

Monet was born in Giverny, France. He began his career drawing caricatures, or cartoonlike figures. He soon switched to painting landscapes and began a lifelong habit of painting outdoors. In 1859, he went to Paris to study art and became friends with the popular artist Camille Pissarro.

In his twenties, Monet served in the French army in Algiers. Army life was not to his liking, and he returned to Paris and began studying art in Gleyre's studio, where he met and befriended Renoir, Alfred Sisley, and other artists of the era. He also studied at the École des Beaux-Arts.

When the Franco-Prussian War threatened Paris life, Monet moved to London. There, he and Pissarro painted Thames River scenes and London parks. When the war ended, Monet returned to France and settled in Argenteuil, a village near Paris.

Monet loved painting *en plein air*—in the open air. When he began work on *Women in the Garden* in 1866, he realized that the size of the canvas created problems. He arranged for a trench to be dug in his backyard. The canvas could be lowered into and raised from the trench by a system of ropes and pulleys. This allowed Monet full access to the entire eight-foot-high canvas.

Monet's best-known works were the series *Haystacks* (1890–1891) and *Waterlilies* (1899). Monet remained committed to the Impressionist movement throughout his life. In his old age, his eyesight failed, but he continued painting until his death in 1926.

Monet's *Wheatstacks, End of Summer* (1890–1891)

Portraits of wealthy women and/or their children helped put food on Renoir's table. *Madame Charpentier and Her Children* (1878) is just such a work.

Impressionism Begins

In 1867 Renoir submitted a painting to the Salon. *Diana, the Huntress*, was almost immediately rejected because the judges felt the topic was crude. Diana was the goddess of the hunt in Roman mythology. The painting was originally a nude, but Renoir realized that the Salon judges did not want nudes. He said, "I did not intend to do anything other than a nude study. But the painting was considered indecent, so I put a bow in the model's hands and a deer at her feet. I added an animal skin to make her nudity less shocking and the painting became a Diana!"[1]

For the next few years, Renoir's life was devoted to painting people. He could not manage to paint people he did not know, so he used his family, friends, and favorite models as subjects in his works. Although he earned little money, his life was carefree. His friends Claude Monet, Alfred Sisley, and other artists painted together, ate together when they had money, and failed together when art sales were few. Under Napoléon III, Parisians enjoyed a renovated city, jobs, and extra money. The wealthy chose to indulge their interests in art, which definitely helped Renoir and his friends.

Then came the Franco-Prussian War, the war that changed Renoir's world. This war pitted France against Prussia, a region in Germany. In 1870, Prussia was an independent country under the guidance of Otto von Bismarck. In July that year, Bismarck led a well-prepared Prussian army against an outnumbered, poorly organized French army. French officers had little experience leading men or developing military plans. Instead, they retreated and were surrounded. Napoléon III quickly surrendered.

During the war, Renoir was drafted into the army. Orders sent him to the Pyrenees Mountains to train horses. That he had no experience with horses did not seem to make a difference to the military. Edgar Degas and Frédéric Bazille also joined the army. Bazille died in action. Rather than join the military, Monet, Sisley, and Pissarro took off for London, and Paul Cézanne went to the south of France. When the war ended in May 1871, Napoléon III resigned and retired to England. The artists gathered back in Paris and resumed painting. The atmosphere that existed before the war had evaporated. Money became scarce, and starving artists continued to starve.

Renoir worked on a new style of painting. Seen up close, the people appeared fuzzy with few clear lines or details. From a distance, his work was stunning. It was about this time that Renoir made his first major sale. A still life brought 400 francs and a landscape called *Pont des Arts* earned 200 francs.

Monet had settled with his wife in the small town of Argenteuil (ar-zhen-TOY) on the Seine River. Renoir spent weeks at Monet's home, where the two artists set up their easels side by side and painted the same subjects from the same perspective. Later in life, the two men could look at those similar paintings and not be able to tell who painted which one. Renoir also painted Monet and Madame Monet reading.

By this time, Renoir turned out canvases with tremendous ease. At times he used fluid brushstrokes. At other times, he slathered on paint with a palette knife. Renoir and Monet developed a technique known as *tache*. *Tache* was single brushstrokes that could be distinguished from other strokes; they captured light on water.

In 1873, Renoir met Paul Durand-Ruel, an art dealer. While many art dealers had been enthusiastic about the new trend in art found in Monet's and Renoir's work, few had sold anything. Durand-Ruel took a more practical approach. As Renoir said, "Enthusiasm is all very well, but it doesn't fill an empty stomach."[2] Through Durand-Ruel, Impressionist works began to sell.

However, few art dealers and critics agreed with Durand-Ruel. In one review, a critic ridiculed the work that Renoir and his friends had put up for sale at an auction. Of Renoir, the critic said, "Try to explain to M. Renoir that woman's torso is not a mass of rotting flesh, with violet-toned green spots all over it, indicating a corpse in the last stages of decay."[3] The auction was a disaster; not one painting sold.

In April 1874, the friends held an exhibit of 163 art works at the studio of Paris photographer Felix Nadar. By this time, the artists were called Impressionists. The works they displayed included watercolors, charcoal sketches, drawings, and pastels. While many came to look at the exhibit, few came to buy. Renoir earned only 18 francs. Critics who attended the exhibit took aim and fired: "The impression that the Impressionists give is of a cat walking on piano keys or a monkey that has taken over a box of paints."[4]

Money grew tight, and Renoir had to lean on his friends for loans. "If you can spare a little money at this time you would make me really happy. I am completely broke," Renoir wrote. In another letter, he said, "I am in trouble this morning for 40 francs, which I do not have. Do you have them or a part? I'll make up the rest by asking other people. But I must find 40 francs before noon and I have exactly 3 francs."[5]

Renoir's father died in 1874 in the house Renoir had purchased in Louveciennes. Renoir, who could barely pay for food and rent at thirty-three years old, went to visit his mother, his sister, and her husband in the house he had purchased at age fifteen.

Desperate, the Impressionists arranged an art sale at the Hôtel Drouot in Paris in the spring of 1875. When the auction began, trouble broke out. People in the crowd booed and yelled during the bidding. The police were called to keep order. The sale was a disaster with one positive aspect. The violence made some people come out in support of the Impressionists. Patrons emerged, and, finally, Renoir began painting on commission.

The life of a workman painter has its ups and downs. Once, Renoir told a friend about taking paintings from one art dealer to another. At every gallery, he heard the same story: Pissarro had just been, and they had bought from him. Art dealers felt sorry for Pissarro because he had so many children to feed. Renoir, however, felt sorry for himself. "Because I am a bachelor and have no children," he complained, "am I to die of starvation?"[6]

It was at this time that Renoir began to distance himself from the Impressionist movement. He painted more "acceptable" works, which he submitted to the official Salon. In 1876, he produced *Le Moulin de la Galette* and

Le Moulin de la Galette (1876) is unusual because of its size (about 52 inches by 70 inches, or 131 cm x 175 cm) and the number of people in the painting. In this work, Renoir captures the sense of being at a party where people chatted, danced, and had fun.

The Swing. In both paintings, Renoir captured the softness and delight of people enjoying themselves. The change was made for practical reasons: He needed to eat and pay his rent.

In 1878 Renoir painted a stunning portrait of Madame Charpentier and her daughters. That painting is now on display at the Metropolitan Museum of Art, New York. The Charpentiers paid him 1,000 francs for the piece. More importantly, they used their influence to help Renoir get his paintings accepted for the yearly Salon.

By this time, Renoir was producing large, salable works. In 1879, he met Aline Charigot. He was thirty-eight to her twenty, and he fell in love with her. Aline worked as a laundress for a seamstress and did Renoir's and Monet's laundry. She became a model for Renoir and is seen in *The Luncheon of the Boating Party*. She is the woman carrying the small dog.

Aline captured Renoir's interest from the start. He courted her by taking her for walks along the Seine. They ate at a local restaurant, then watched people row on the water, or Aline swam. At night, they listened to music. Renoir later described Aline's dancing to his son Jean: "[She] waltzed divinely. . . . The star dancer [at the café] was Barbier. When he started whirling your mother around, everybody stopped to watch them."[7] Several years passed before Renoir decided he simply could not live without Aline, and in 1890 he married her.

In *The Swing* (1876), Renoir creates the effect of sunlight sifting through leaves. The model was Jeanne Samary, a popular French actress in the late 1800s. Splashes of light on Jeanne's dress give the viewer a sense of an afternoon in summer.

In 1881 Renoir traveled to Algiers because he had heard it was a place of many shades of white. He wrote to art dealer Durand-Ruel, "I wanted to see what the land of sun was like. I am out of luck, for there is scarcely any at the moment. But it is exquisite all the same, an extraordinary wealth of nature."[8] Surprisingly, several of Renoir's Algerian paintings were not painted in Algiers. His Algerian women were studio paintings of Paris models.

The Luncheon of the Boating Party (1880–1882) is considered one of Renoir's finest works. The atmosphere is relaxed; the people full of food and wine. The woman holding the dog in the foreground is Renoir's future wife, Aline.

By 1883, Renoir found himself in a personal crisis. He lacked self-confidence in his talent. Looking back on that time, he wrote, "About 1883, a kind of crisis occurred in my work. I had gone to the end of Impressionism and I was reaching the conclusion that I didn't know how either to paint or to draw. In a word, I was at a dead end."[9]

Napoléon III

France in the 1840s was a city of narrow, dark alleys, pockets of poverty, and unemployed workmen. The government was under the control of King Louis Philippe; his queen was Marie-Amélie. The upper class lived privileged, elegant, comfortable lives. The lower classes lived in filth and despair. Hunger, disease, and hopelessness affected the majority of the French people. Those people usually could not read or write and had no opportunities to earn money or improve their lives.

On February 22, 1848, the working class rose up in a revolution. The streets of Paris became the site of bloody battles. The rioters forced King Louis Philippe to give up his crown and flee to England. The French people elected a new government called the National Constituent Assembly. Charles-Louis-Napoléon Bonaparte, a relative of the original Napoléon Bonaparte, ran for election to the assembly and won. He became president of the Second Republic.

Three years later, Charles-Louis-Napoléon Bonaparte seized power, becoming a dictator. He named himself Napoléon III, Emperor of the French and leader of the Second Empire. Napoléon III ruled from 1852 to 1870, when he surrendered during the Franco-Prussian War. From the beginning, he became involved in France's economic growth.

The greatest problem facing France at the time was unemployment. Emperor Napoléon worked hard to develop industries and create new jobs. He promoted a vast rebuilding of Paris, replacing slums with broad boulevards and open squares. A national railroad connected Paris to the rest of France. These major building programs employed hundreds of workers.

During his reign, Napoléon III slowly restored democracy to France.

Napoléon III (Charles-Louis-Napoléon Bonaparte) served as president of the French Republic from 1848 to 1851, and as Emperor of the French from 1852 to 1870. He was the last monarch of France.

He gave up holding absolute power by transferring his power to the elected legislature. By 1870, the government was able to run the country without an emperor, and Napoléon III gave up his throne. He moved to England and died there three years later, in 1873.

The Artist's Family (1896) features Renoir's wife, Aline, and the couple's children. Aline, pictured in many Renoir works, is dressed up for the occasion and seems a bit uncomfortable in her fine clothes.

CHAPTER 4

four

Moving On Alone

Renoir and Monet went on their last painting trip together in 1883. The two old friends were heading down different paths. Monet maintained his dedication to Impressionism. Renoir sought something different. He wanted to find what he called "greater harmonies" in his painting.

Renoir entered his Harsh (or Dry) Period. He now painted in the studio rather than outdoors. His style became more formal, more traditional, yet he was still not satisfied. "I am still obsessed with experimenting. I'm not satisfied and I erase and I keep erasing. I hope this obsession passes. I am like children at school. . . . I am forty years old and I'm still sketching."[1]

Two works that show this change in Renoir's style are *Dance in the Country* and *Dance in the City.* These paintings are large, with clearly drawn figures. *Dance in the Country* features Aline as the model. It is a picture of a woman in the arms of her partner. The viewer gets the feeling of a delighted couple swirling to the music. The picture is natural, comfortable, and shows pure enjoyment, similar to Renoir's earlier works.

Renoir's son Jean said of his father, "Each stage of life was for him marked by amazing discoveries. He looked at the world with continual astonishment, a feeling of surprise which he made no effort to hide."[2]

It seemed, however, that the joy of life had been drained from Renoir's art of the Harsh Period. *Dance in the City* gives the viewer a look at the new style. The picture is cold, icy, and formal. It is more typical of Renoir's attitude toward his life during that time.

Looking at Renoir's body of work, it is obvious that he had changing interests, changing approaches to his subjects. Between 1870 and 1880,

27

Dance in the City and *Dance in the Country* (1883) contrast two similar scenes. In the city, dancing is obviously an elegant affair, but the country scene shows the delight of the dancers. Both paintings are life-size, with little room for anything except the central figures.

Renoir painted few nude studies. In 1883, his differing approach brought him back to nude figures. In that year, he began *Great Bathers*, a painting that took several years to finish. The style of this work is freer, more classical, more defined, and yet it is still Renoir.

No longer a member of the Impressionists, Renoir thought about starting a new society of artists. He wrote in his notebook: "I propose to found a society. It is to be called 'The Society of Irregulars.' The members would have to know that a circle should never be round."[3] While this may have been a joke, Renoir was serious about solid relationships with fellow artists.

One particularly valued friendship began for Renoir at the Hôtel Drouot and the exhibition that ended in violence. At that exhibition, Renoir met Gustave Caillebotte, a wealthy young artist. Caillebotte not only painted, but he also supported a number of artists by buying their works for his collection.

As early as 1879, Caillebotte had a will drawn up for which Renoir was executor. Selected pieces from Caillebotte's collection would be donated to the government. Among the artists represented in this gift were Édouard Manet, Monet, Renoir, and Cézanne. The one condition to Caillebotte's gift was that the art be displayed at the Louvre Museum. This idea caused quite a problem. The formal side of the French art community—the École des Beaux-Arts and the French Institute—still rejected the Impressionists' work. They controlled what was shown in French museums. Because of the strings attached, Caillebotte's gift was not gladly received.

In 1885, Renoir began a new career: father. Aline gave birth to a son, Pierre, on March 23 that year. Caillebotte agreed to serve as Pierre's godfather. At the time, Renoir and Aline were living in rooms attached to Renoir's studio. Aline suggested that they consider a bigger apartment so that a crying baby would not disturb Renoir's work. The family moved into a four-room apartment only a few blocks away from the studio.

Pierre was a lovely, healthy baby. His sweet face looks out from many of Renoir's works done during Pierre's youth. One study, *Nursing*, shows Aline nursing baby Pierre. The child is plump and round; the presentation tender and emotional. This piece shows Renoir's deep affection for both mother and child.

After seven years in the Harsh Period, Renoir looked back with sadness. "I find everything I've done ugly and it would be all the more painful to me to see it exhibited."[4] In about 1890, Renoir reinvented himself again. This time, he entered the Iridescent Period, which featured glowing, pearly colors, mellow textures, and soft brushstrokes.

Renoir loved painting his wife, Aline. In this picture, *Mother Nursing Her Child* (1886), Aline appears soft and loving as she nurses the couple's son, Pierre.

By this point, Aline had been an important part of Renoir's life for many years, and he decided to make the arrangement official. The two married in a civil ceremony on April 14, 1890. Marriage did not change their lives much. Renoir continued to paint and pursue his friendships. Aline cared for their home and child.

The 1892 painting called *Two Young Girls at the Piano* is typical of Renoir's Iridescent Period. The painting shows a young girl seated at a piano. She is dressed in white and has blond hair and fresh, rosy skin. Another girl, dark-haired and rosy cheeked, leans near the first. The picture features varied shades of reds, roses, yellows, and oranges. Light dances on the girls' hair and cheeks, creating a glow.

In addition to painting many scenes with young girls, Renoir continued to use Aline as a model, often showing her with young Pierre. The picture *Aline and Pierre* (also called *Washerwoman and Baby*) is a sweet, soft pastel drawing showing the mother kissing her son on his cheek. The picture is typical of Renoir's approach to painting women.

Renoir was fascinated by the actions of women and portrayed them doing normal, "female" activities: washing clothes, minding children, bathing, walking in the park, and picking apples. It is obvious that Renoir admired husky women. All his models are fleshy, plump beauties. They generally have small noses, wide full-lipped mouths, and light complexions. Oddly, Renoir had been painting these features for years before meeting Aline—a woman who was the prime example of everything Renoir considered beautiful.

Many of Renoir's paintings done during the 1890s feature young girls. This one, *Two Young Girls at the Piano* (1892), focuses on a common event in daily life: piano practice.

In 1892, Renoir at last agreed to another exhibit. Art dealer Durand-Ruel sponsored the show, which featured 110 paintings and was the largest one-man exhibit of Impressionist works. Included were several major pieces: *Le Moulin de la Galette*, *Luncheon of the Boating Party*, and *The Bathers*. Everything displayed was a tribute to Renoir's talent and vision. The exhibit showed pastels, watercolors, sketches, and oil paintings. The work ranged from landscapes and seascapes to nudes, from children at play to women at work. Even the techniques used to produce the paintings differed. Some showed soft, delicate brushstrokes and smooth textures; others portrayed the drama created by swaths of paint laid on with a palette knife. Throughout the works, Renoir's love of common events and brilliant colors dominated. The exhibition was a success, and Renoir was acclaimed a master, a title he despised.

Early in 1894, Renoir's friend Caillebotte died, and his will became a source of argument in the art world. As the will's executor, Renoir helped choose sixty works of art to be displayed in the Louvre, according to the provisions of the will. However, the Louvre was dedicated to fine art. Works by Impressionists were not yet considered fine art, and Caillebotte's gift was viewed without enthusiasm. Renoir compromised at forty paintings; the Louvre grit its collective teeth and accepted. The rest of Caillebotte's collection remained as property of his family. Less than 100 years later, Caillebotte's collection would have been worth more than $100 million. Most of the works donated are now in the Musée d'Orsay in Paris, a museum dedicated to nineteenth- and twentieth-century art.

Later that year, Aline and Auguste welcomed another son, Jean [ZHAW(n)]. Renoir's workload was so heavy that he felt he could not offer Aline enough help with the children. He brought cousin Gabrielle Renard to live in the Renoir home and serve as governess. At the time, Gabrielle was a mere teenager. Later, she became one of Renoir's favorite models. Gabrielle, like Aline, was soft-looking, sweet, and lively.

Gabrielle is seen in the painting *The Artist's Family*. Renoir shows Aline as plump and matronly in an overly fussy hat, print blouse, and ample skirt. Pierre, twelve years old, wears a sailor's suit, an outfit common for boys in 1896. Jean is a toddler, dressed in the typical clothing for boys and girls: a dress and bonnet.

Renoir's life settled into an easy pace. He painted. Aline and Gabrielle cared for the children. The family traveled to the seashore, or Renoir went on painting trips. Renoir's art sold well; money was plentiful.

That calm existence would soon come to an end.

The Louvre

The Louvre Museum houses many of the world's greatest artworks. However, it was not built to be a museum but a fortress. In about 1200, King Philippe Auguste's advisers suggested he build a fort to guard the entrance to Paris along the Seine River. King Philippe Auguste headed off to the Crusades in the Middle East while his builders erected the Louvre. At times the Louvre served as a prison, a vault for the French king's jewels, and an armory for keeping weapons. It came equipped with a rather bleak dungeon.

When Charles V became king in 1364, he converted the fortress into his personal library. The old, dark fort got a makeover that added windows, a grand staircase, and better housing for the royal family.

François I started the idea of using the Louvre as a museum in the 1500s with a small collection of twelve paintings. These included works by Italian Renaissance artists Titian, Raphael, and Leonardo da Vinci. Until the French Revolution in 1789, the Louvre was a private museum for the royal family and guests. In 1793, the Louvre was opened to the public and underwent a name change: It became the Museum of the Republic. Parisians, however, continued to call it the Louvre. It was at the Louvre that Renoir studied the works of Watteau, Boucher, and Fragonard.

By 2007, the Louvre owned nearly 300,000 pieces, including works by such famous artists as Renoir, Michelangelo, Rembrandt, Albrecht Dürer, Jan Vermeer, and Sir Joshua Reynolds. Leonardo da Vinci's *Mona Lisa (La Joconde)* may be the museum's most famous and most visited work of art. Only a small percentage of those works are on display at any time. More than 8 million people visited the Louvre in 2006.

The Louvre Museum at night

As age and arthritis advanced, Renoir had to make changes in his life. He moved about in a wheelchair but was still able to paint. He developed a leather mitt to help him hold his brushes despite the crippling effects of arthritis in his hands.

five

Renoir's Last Years

Auguste and Aline Renoir began to face new difficulties. Aline felt tired and run down. Her doctor diagnosed diabetes. The discovery that insulin helped control diabetes had not yet been made. Doctors could only suggest restricted diets, and Aline liked her food too much to watch what she ate.

Auguste began to feel great pain in his hands. His doctor said he had rheumatoid arthritis, which affects the joints. The condition eventually deformed his hands, curling them inward and crippling his fingers. That did not stop him from painting.

As the twentieth century began, only four of the original Impressionists still lived: Degas, Pissarro, Monet, and Renoir. Degas, in his late sixties, was losing his eyesight. No longer able to paint, he turned to sculpture. Pissarro continued to exhibit works up until his death in 1903. Monet was sixty in 1900. He, too, was losing his eyesight and had become obsessed with painting scenes of the lily pond on his property in Giverny, France. Renoir's health was rapidly failing due to the increasing pain of his arthritis.

In 1900, Renoir received word that he had been named chevalier of the Legion of Honor. Such awards did not impress him, and he sent a representative to Paris to receive the honor in his place. He had greater demands at home. Aline's health was not good, and she was pregnant with their third child. Claude, called Coco, was born in August 1901.

Doctors continued to treat Renoir's condition, but it seemed hopeless. Slowly, his hands became so deformed that his fingers curled into his palms. He lost weight, and, by 1904, weighed only 105 pounds. Paris winters affected him badly, and his doctors recommended that he move to the South of

Renoir's handling of these two girls in *Two Sisters* (1881) is filled with light. The older girl's red hat draws the viewer's eye. Note that the background is vague and indistinct compared to the detail in the young girl's hat in the foreground.

France, where winters are milder.

In 1905, Aline, Auguste, and family moved to Cagnes-sur-Mer, a small town overlooking the Mediterranean Sea. At first, the Renoirs lived in an apartment attached to the post office. Two years later, Auguste bought an estate just outside of town, called Les Collettes. The land boasted an olive grove, an orange grove, and many gardens. Renoir had a house built, complete with an art studio nestled among the olive trees.

In an interview with American Walter Pach in 1908, Renoir talked about his painting. He told Pach, "I arrange my subject as I want it, then I go ahead and paint it, like a child . . . I am no cleverer than that. . . . Shall I tell you what I think are the two qualities of art? It must be indescribable and it must be inimitable. . . . The work of art must seize upon you, wrap you up in itself, carry you away."[1]

In 1908, Renoir decided to do as Degas had and make an attempt at sculpture. His hands were so knotted that he could not lift a mallet to tap stone or shape clay. Instead, he hired Spanish artist Ricardo Guino to be his hands. Renoir sketched the statues he wanted created. Guino converted the sketches into art under Renoir's careful direction. Renoir was, by this time, in a wheelchair. He would move it around the statue, inspecting every detail. "Take a bit off there . . . a little more . . . that's right! This should be rounder, fuller. . . ."[2] With his attention on every inch of the sculpture, Renoir directed

Guino's every movement. The statues, like many of Renoir's later works, were nude figures.

Renoir continued to paint through the pain. He could not hold a brush, so he devised a leather harness for his hand to hold the brush for him. His painting *Vines at Cagnes*, or *The Vineyard*, is one of Renoir's later landscapes, painted using the harness. He found getting the light and the color of olive trees quite a challenge. He wrote to a friend: "The olive tree, what a brute! If you realized how much trouble it has caused me. A tree full of colors. Not great at all. Its little leaves, how they've made me sweat! . . . I know I can't paint nature, but I enjoy struggling with it. A painter can't be great if he doesn't understand landscape."[3]

Renoir loved the light, airy nature of the Mediterranean town of Cagnes. The *Terrace in Cagnes* (1905) is bright and sunny, with an abundance of whites and yellows.

Daily living placed greater demands on Renoir. He needed assistance for even the simplest chores of an average day. He could not get out of bed without help, nor dress or feed himself. The pain was so great that even the weight of blankets put him in agony. A wire cage was made and placed over Renoir when in bed. His blankets lay over the cage. He wore baggy trousers, a gray jacket, and a white straw hat. Because he no longer walked anywhere, he preferred soft carpet slippers to stronger, hard-soled shoes. His hair had grown stark white and his beard long and scruffy.

Despite his pain, he loved life. His eyesight remained keen, and he delighted in the many greens that played in the olive grove, as well as in the yellow, pink, and purple wildflowers on the area's hillsides. Money was no longer an issue for Renoir. His paintings sold well, but he remained a simple man. He preferred beans and potatoes to eating caviar; his frayed wool coat to lush velvets.

In 1912, Renoir traveled to Paris in his chauffeur-driven car. There, he met with old friends. Shocked to see him in such frail health, they called in well-known medical experts to help Renoir. A doctor was brought from Vienna, Austria, and, after an examination, promised to get Renoir back on his feet in a matter of weeks. He ordered a specific diet to build Renoir's strength. Renoir agreed and followed the diet exactly. A month later, the doctor said Renoir was ready to walk. He helped Renoir to his feet and told him to take a step. Renoir took one step, then another. He slowly walked around his easel, then back toward his wheelchair.

"I give up," he said. "It takes all my will-power and I would have none left for painting. . . . If I have to choose between walking and painting, I'd much rather paint."[4] He returned to his wheelchair, and remained wheelchair-bound for the rest of his life.

In the May 6, 1914, edition of the *Paris-Journal*, Renoir was declared "the greatest living painter."[5] This honor was not one that Renoir welcomed. He still considered himself a "workman" painter and was embarrassed to be classed among the great masters.

Within months, events took place that dramatically changed the Renoirs' lives. The Archduke Franz Ferdinand of Austro-Hungary was murdered in Sarajevo. Through a chain of alliances, France found itself at war. Pierre was

The hardest subject for an artist to paint is himself.
No one sees himself as others do. In this self-portrait,
painted in 1910, Renoir captures both the aging in his
face and the spark of life in his eyes.

already in the military reserve; Jean signed up for the army. Both sons were
wounded early in the fighting. Pierre's arm was so badly damaged that he left
the military. Jean healed and returned to the battlefront. In 1915, a German
bullet shattered his leg.

Jean arrived in a Paris hospital in terrible condition. Aline left Cagnes to see how her son was doing. She arrived just before the surgeons were preparing to cut off Jean's leg. His wound had developed gangrene. Aline insisted that Jean's leg be treated and not removed. She helped nurse her son and returned to Cagnes only after she was sure the leg had been saved.

Aline returned home and died of a heart attack the next day. She was only fifty-one, but untreated diabetes and poor eating habits had weakened her heart. The stress of caring for her son had brought on an early death.

Renoir was devastated to lose her. To work through his feelings, he began to paint fanatically, as if he could paint over his grief. Physically, he became even weaker, eating little, sleeping in pain, and speaking so softly that he could barely be heard.

In 1919, Renoir was named a commander of the Legion of Honor, an award given to famous French citizens. A newspaper reported that Renoir went to Paris and the Louvre for the last time, carried around "like a pope on his throne."[6] He visited the pictures of his past, saying farewell to Delacroix, Fragonard, Boucher, Watteau, and da Vinci. In November he caught pneumonia, yet he had at least one more piece left to paint—a still life of apples.

By December Renoir had to keep to his room. His lungs were infected, and he was growing steadily weaker. He painted flowers collected for him by the maid. When he was finished, he said, "I think I am beginning to understand something about it."[7] He was referring to art.

Renoir died on December 3, 1919. He left his three sons an estate valued at 5 million francs, along with 720 paintings. Renoir was buried beside Aline in a cemetery in Essoyes, France, where Aline had lived as a child.

In 1920, three major exhibits of Renoir's works honored the artist. Today, just one of his paintings sells for millions of dollars. His work is exhibited in major art museums throughout the world. Renoir's close friend, Georges Riviére, wrote:

You could, O Renoir, leave us without sadness.
The treasures generously sown by your brush
Will make your name live long after you have gone.[8]

World War I

In 1914, a Serbian rebel shot and killed Archduke Franz Ferdinand of Austro-Hungary. Ferdinand's death sparked a war that spread around the globe: World War I. Ferdinand was heir to the Austro-Hungarian throne, but he was not popular. Still, Austro-Hungary could not ignore the murder of one of their royal family.

Austro-Hungary sent a strongly worded note demanding punishment for those involved in the attack. If Serbia did not meet Austro-Hungary's demands, the Austrians planned a quick, tidy, local war. The one worry Austro-Hungary had was Russia. Russia and Serbia had a pact to protect each other. To be safe, Austro-Hungary checked with its friend Germany to see whether Germany would jump in on their side if Russia stepped in to help Serbia.

Basically, World War I went from a small event to a global war because of friendships, relatives, and treaties. Serbia had a treaty with Russia; Russia was allied to France. On the other side, Austro-Hungary was tied to Germany, and Germany's Otto von Bismarck welcomed a war. Bismarck felt Germany could expand its power in Europe and used the war with Serbia to overrun smaller European countries, such as Belgium. A treaty with Belgium brought Great Britain into the war. Ties to Britain brought

Otto von Bismarck

Japan, Australia, Canada, India, New Zealand, and the Union of South Africa into what would be called World War I.

The war was a brutal, four-year conflict. Men fought, ate, and slept in deep trenches on both sides of the front lines. Submarines, tanks, and chemical weapons were used for the first time during the war. Renoir's sons, Pierre and Jean, were both seriously injured during the conflict.

1841	Pierre-Auguste Renoir is born in Limoges, France, on February 25.
1845	Auguste and his family move to Paris.
1854	Auguste becomes an apprentice painter of porcelain.
1858	After the porcelain company closes, Renoir begins painting fans.
1861	The artist enrolls in Gleyre's studio and meets Monet, Sisley, and Bazille.
1862	He enrolls at the École des Beaux-Arts.
1866	Renoir paints *At the Inn of Mother Anthony*.
1869	Monet and Renoir paint together at Bougival.
1873	Monet and Renoir work together at Argenteuil on the banks of the Seine.
1874	Auguste takes part in the first group exhibition of the Impressionists. Léonard Renoir dies.
1876	Renoir takes part in a second exhibition of work; he paints several portraits.
1878	Renoir paints *Madame Charpentier and Her Children*.
1880	Aline Charigot, later Mme. Renoir, is part of the group in the painting *The Luncheon of the Boating Party*.
1881	The artist departs for Algeria in the spring and Italy in the fall.
1883	Renoir breaks with Impressionism; Harsh Period begins.
1885	Son Pierre is born.
1890	Renoir begins Iridescent Period. He and Aline marry.
1894	Second son, Jean, is born; Renoir family moves to Montmartre in Paris.
1896	Renoir's mother dies.
1898	He suffers his first serious attack of arthritis.
1900	Renoir takes part in a major art show at the Paris World's Fair. He is named chevalier of the French Legion of Honor.
1901	Third son, Claude, called Coco, is born.
1907	Renoir moves permanently to Les Collettes in Cagnes-sur-Mer.
1908	Arthritis and rheumatism force Renoir to begin using a wheelchair, but he does not stop painting.
1912	Wheelchair-bound, he begins sculpting with the help of Ricardo Guino.
1914–1915	Pierre and Jean are both wounded in World War I. Aline Renoir dies.
1919	Renoir dies at Cagnes on December 3.

SELECTED WORKS

1864	*Esmeralda Dancing with a Goat*
1866	*At the Inn of Mother Anthony*
1867	*Lise with a Parasol*
	Diana, the Huntress
	Pont des Arts
1870	*Odalisque*
	Woman in a Park
1873	*Monet Painting in his Garden at Argenteuil*
	A Morning Ride in the Bois de Boulogne
1874	*La Loge*
	Sailboats at Argenteuil
	Madame Monet with Her Son
	The Dancer
	The Parisian
1875	*Portrait of Claude Monet*
	Woman with a Cat
	Lady at the Piano
1876	*Self Portrait*
	Portrait of Victor Chocquet
	A Girl with a Watering-Can
	Le Moulin de la Galette
	The Swing
1878	*Madame Charpentier and Her Children*
	Young Women Talking
1879	*Two Little Circus Girls*
	Oarsman at Chatou
1880–1882	*Luncheon of the Boating Party*
1881–1886	*The Umbrellas*
	Two Sisters (On the Terrace)
1883	*Dance in the Country/ Country Dance (Aline Charigot and Paul Lhote)*
	Dance in the City/City Dance
1884	*Children's Afternoon at Wargemont*
1885	*Bather Arranging Her Hair*
1886	*Mother Nursing Her Child (Aline and Pierre)*
1887	*Bathers*
1892	*Two Young Girls at the Piano*
1896	*The Artist's Family*
1903	*Variant of the Bathers*
1906	*The Promenade*
1908	*Vines at Cagnes/The Vineyard*
1910	*Self-Portrait*
1918	*The Bathers*

1815	Napoléon Bonaparte is defeated at Waterloo, ending Bonaparte's rule in France.
1833	Victor Hugo publishes *The Hunchback of Notre Dame*.
1841	U.S. President Harrison dies after only one month in office.
1844	Morse sends the first telegraph message, "What hath God wrought!"
1846	Elias Howe patents a lock-stitch sewing machine.
1848	The February Revolution in France ousts King Louis Philippe.
1849	The California gold rush encourages settlement in the western United States.
1850	The first official women's medical college in the United States opens in Pennsylvania.
1852	Charles-Louis-Napoléon Bonaparte names himself Emperor of the French.
1853	Chicago, Illinois, and the U.S. east coast are connected by railroad for the first time.
1854	France, Great Britain, and Turkey declare war on Russia, beginning the Crimean War.
1855	Samuel Martin Kier builds America's first oil refinery in Pittsburgh, Pennsylvania.
1859	Work begins on the Suez Canal, a channel that will connect the Mediterranean Sea with the Indian Ocean.
1861	The U.S. Civil War begins.
1865	General Robert E. Lee surrenders to General Ulysses S. Grant, ending the Civil War.
1867	The British North America Act establishes the Dominion of Canada.
1870–1871	The Franco-Prussian War is fought.
1872	Monet paints *Impression: Sunrise*.
1876	Alexander Graham Bell patents the first telephone.
1878	Thomas Edison patents the first phonograph.
1884	Mark Twain publishes *The Adventures of Huckleberry Finn*.
1889	The first celluloid film in the U.S., *Fred Ott's Sneeze*, is made.
1896	The modern Olympics are held for the first time in Athens, Greece.
1903	Orville and Wilbur Wright launch a successful manned flight in a motorized airplane.
1909	The National Association for the Advancement of Colored People (NAACP) is founded in New York.
1911	Roald Amundsen's expedition reaches the South Pole.
1914	World War I begins when the Archduke Franz Ferdinand is assassinated.
1918	Fighting ends in World War I; a treaty will follow in a year.
1939–1945	World War II envelops Europe and Asia.

CHAPTER NOTES

Chapter 1. A Painter's Legacy
1. Barbara Ehrlich White, *Renoir: His Life, Art, and Letters* (New York: Harry N. Abrams, Inc., 1984), p. 51.
2. Denis Rouart, *Renoir* (New York: Rizzoli International Publications, 1985), p. 114.
3. Ibid., p. 115.
4. Margherita d'Ayala Valva and Alexander Auf der Heyde, eds., *Renoir* (New York: Rizzoli International Publications, Inc., 2005), p. 23.
5. White, p. 217.

Chapter 2. Learning His Craft
1. Jean Renoir, Renoir, *My Father* (Boston: Little, Brown, and Company, 1962), p. 71.
2. Diane Kelder, *The Great Book of French Impressionism* (New York: Abbeville Press, 1997), p. 202.
3. Ibid., p. 201.

Chapter 3. Impressionism Begins
1. Margherita d'Ayala Valva and Alexander Auf der Heyde, eds., *Renoir* (New York: Rizzoli International Publications, Inc., 2005), p. 31.
2. Jean Renoir, *Renoir, My Father* (Boston: Little, Brown, and Company, 1962), p. 157.
3. Ibid., p. 159.
4. D'Ayala Valva and Auf der Heyde, p. 43.
5. Barbara Ehrlich White, *Renoir: His Life, Art, and Letters* (New York: Harry N. Abrams, Inc., 1984), p. 54.
6. Ibid., p. 79.
7. Jean Renoir, p. 217.
8. Pierre-Auguste Renoir and Rachel Barnes, *Artists by Themselves: Renoir* (New York: Alfred A. Knopf, Inc., 1990), p. 44.
9. Ibid., p. 10.

Chapter 4. Moving On Alone
1. Margherita d'Ayala Valva and Alexander Auf der Heyde, eds., *Renoir* (New York: Rizzoli International Publications, Inc., 2005), p. 55.
2. Jean Renoir, *Renoir, My Father* (Boston: Little, Brown, and Company, 1962), p. 38.
3. Ibid., p. 245.
4. D'Ayala and Auf der Heyde, p. 58.

Chapter 5. Renoir's Last Years
1. Margherita d'Ayala Valva and Alexander Auf der Heyde, eds., *Renoir* (New York: Rizzoli International Publications, Inc., 2005), p. 66.
2. Peter H. Feist, *Pierre-Auguste Renoir* (New York: Taschen, 2000), p. 78.
3. Pierre-Auguste Renoir and Rachel Barnes, *Artists by Themselves: Renoir* (New York: Alfred A. Knopf, Inc., 1990), p. 66.
4. Jean Renoir, *Renoir, My Father* (Boston: Little, Brown, and Company, 1962), p. 446.
5. Barbara Ehrlich White, *Renoir: His Life, Art, and Letters* (New York: Harry N. Abrams, Inc., 1984), p. 271.
6. Francesca Castellani, *Renoir: His Life and Works* (Philadelphia: Courage Books, 1998), p. 31.
7. Jean Renoir, p. 458.
8. Georges Riviére, "Sonnet to Renoir," unpublished poem, 1920; quoted in White, p. 285.

For Young Adults

De Varvalho, Roberto. *Impressionism.* New York: Peter Bedrick Books, 2003.

D'Harcourt, Claire. *Masterpieces Up Close: Western Painting from the 14th to 20th Centuries.* San Francisco: Chronicle Books, 2006.

Frey, Lisa Alexandra. *The Story of Monet and Renoir.* Quogue, NY: Starshell Press, 2004.

Lacey, Sue. *In the Time of Renoir.* Silver Spring, MD: Sagebrush, 2002.

Pach, Walter. *Renoir: Master of Art.* New York: Harry N. Abrams, 2003.

Spence, David. *Renoir.* Hauppauge, NY: Barron's Educational Series, 1998.

Raimondo, Joyce. *Picture This! Activities and Adventures in Impressionism.* New York: Watson-Guptill, 2004.

Venezia, Mike. *Pierre Auguste Renoir.* Silver Spring, MD: Sagebrush, 2001.

Welton, Jude. *Impressionism.* New York: DK Publishing, 2000.

Works Consulted

Benjamin, Roger. *Renoir and Algeria.* Williamston, MA: The Clark Institute, 2003.

Castellani, Francesca. *Renoir: His Life and Works.* Philadelphia: Courage Books, 1998.

D'Ayala Valva, Margherita, and Alexander Auf der Heyde, eds. *Renoir.* New York: Rizzoli International Publications, Inc., 2005.

Feist, Peter H. *Renoir.* New York: Taschen, 2000.

Kelder, Diane. *The Great Book of French Impressionism.* New York: Abbeville Press, 1997.

Neret, Gilles. *Renoir: The Painter of Happiness.* New York: Taschen, 2001.

Renoir, Jean. *Renoir: My Father.* Boston: Little, Brown, and Company, 1962.

Renoir, Pierre-Auguste, and Rachel Barnes. *Artists by Themselves: Renoir.* New York: Alfred A. Knopf, Inc., 1990.

Rouart, Denis. *Renoir.* New York: Rizzoli International Publications, Inc., 1985.

White, Barbara Ehrlich. *Renoir: His Life, Art, and Letters.* New York: Harry N. Abrams, Inc., 1984.

On the Internet

Auguste Renoir Paintings Gallery, "Auguste Renoir"
http://www.renoir.org.yu/

Getty Museum, "Pierre-Auguste Renoir"
http://www.getty.edu/art/gettyguide/art MakerDetails?maker=620

Olga's Gallery, "Pierre-Auguste Renoir"
http://abcgallery.com/R/renoir/ renoir.html

The Online Renoir Museum, "Pierre-Auguste Renoir (1841–1919)"
http://www.expo-renoir.com/

"Pierre-Auguste Renoir"
http://www.chez.com/renoir/indexe.html

"Pierre-Auguste Renoir Online"
http://www.artcyclopedia.com/artists/ renoir_pierre-auguste.html

WebMuseum, "Pierre-Auguste Renoir"
http://www.ibiblio.org/wm/paint/auth/ renoir/

GLOSSARY

apprentice (uh-PREN-tis)
A student who works with a master in order to learn a skill.

commercial art (kuh-MUR-shul art)
Art done for business purposes, such as painting plates or vases or designing ads or posters.

commission (kuh-MIH-shun)
Being hired to do a particular piece of work.

executor (ek-SEH-kyoo-tur)
The person appointed to carry out the instructions left in a will.

forgery (FOR-juh-ree)
A false document or artwork presented as being done by someone else.

inimitable (in-IM-ih-tah-bul)
Impossible to imitate, especially because of being unique to a particular person or group.

iridescent (ee-rih-DEH-sent)
Shiny or glowing, such as a pearl.

lithograph (LIH-thuh-graf)
A copy produced by printing.

medium (MEE-dee-um)
A material used to produce art, such as chalk, oil paint, or watercolor.

palette (PAA-let)
A board on which an artist places oil or acrylic paints to make them accessible during the process of painting.

porcelain (POR-suh-len)
A nearly clear type of fine ceramic used to make dishes, vases, and lamps.

portrait (POR-tret)
A painting or photograph of a person, usually showing the face.

print
A piece of art that has been printed or duplicated from an original.

rheumatoid arthritis (ROO-mah-toyd ar-THRYE-tis)
A disease that causes pain, stiffness, and swelling in the joints; it can eventually destroy the joints.

sous (SOO)
A French coin having little value.